CHRISTMAS CRAFTERS

DECORATIONS & CRAFTS

TO MAKE YOUR CHRISTMAS MERRY

By Charlene Olexiewicz

Illustrated by Dianne O'Quinn Burke
Photographs by Ann Bogart

Lowell 🏠 House
Juvenile
Los Angeles

CONTEMPORARY BOOKS
Chicago

NOTE: The numbered stars above the heading of each craft indicates the level of difficulty; one star being the easiest, three stars being the hardest.

Publisher: Jack Artenstein
Associate Publisher, Juvenile Division: Elizabeth Amos
Director of Publishing Services: Rena Copperman
Managing Editor, Juvenile Division: Lindsey Hay
Editor in Chief, Juvenile Division, Nonfiction: Amy Downing
Art Director: Lisa-Theresa Lenthall
Typesetting: Justin Segal
Crafts Artist: Charlene Olexiewicz
Models: Carly Seibel, page 5; Danielle Seibel, page 17

Library of Congress Catalog Card Number is available.

ISBN: 1-56565-492-7

Lowell House books can be purchased at special discounts when ordered in bulk for premiums and special sales. Contact Department JH at the following address:

Lowell House Juvenile
2020 Avenue of the Stars, Suite 300
Los Angeles, CA 90067

Manufactured in the United States of America
10 9 8 7 6 5 4 3 2 1

CONTENTS

HAPPY HOLIDAY NECKLACE

WHAT YOU'LL NEED

- 60 inches of white cord
- clear tape
- ruler
- scissors
- red and green embroidery floss
- assorted buttons
- wooden beads
- assorted Christmas charms
- gold metallic thread

DIRECTIONS

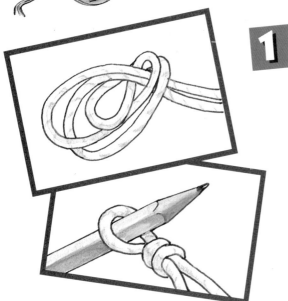

1 Wrap the two ends of white cord with clear tape to keep them from unraveling. Double cord in half so that the ends meet evenly. At the looped end, tie a knot, leaving a loop large enough for a regular pencil to slide through freely.

2 Starting at the looped end, line up two cords, side by side. Beginning at knot, measure 3 inches and make another knot, joining the two cords together. Repeat this until there are nine knots in all, each 3 inches apart. Take the two free ends, thread them through the loop, and tie one final knot, closing the necklace. Cut off any excess cord.

3 Using red and green embroidery floss, tie on buttons, beads, and charms to the three center sections of cord, so they're hanging down ½ inch to 1 inch. Once an item is tied, trim off excess floss that is longer than 1 inch. Continue until the three sections are full on *both* cords.

4 For extra sparkle, 8-inch lengths of gold metallic thread can be tied in double-knotted bows and scattered throughout. You'll have so much fun creating your holiday necklace that you'll want to make another for Mom or that special Sunday school teacher.

A SPECIAL CHRISTMAS TOUCH

If you really want to get in the Christmas spirit, make a bracelet to match. Just follow the same directions, measuring it about one-third to half the length of your necklace.

Add some pizzazz to your favorite red or green outfit with this charming holiday accessory!

JINGLE BELL FRAME

WHAT YOU'LL NEED

- compass
- paper
- 6-by-6-inch green or white plastic canvas
- stapler
- scissors
- green yarn
- needle with large eye
- ¼-inch-wide red satin ribbon, 2 yards
- red thread
- twenty sleigh bells (³⁄₈-inch size)
- cardboard
- ruler
- craft glue

DIRECTIONS

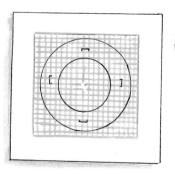

1 Using a compass, on a piece of paper draw a 3-inch circle centered inside a 5-inch circle. Trace over lines using a dark-color marker. Take the plastic canvas and cut a small hole at the center, about ½ inch wide. Place plastic canvas on top of paper.

2 Staple canvas to the paper, keeping staples inside wreath shape. With scissors, cut out wreath shape, using the paper guidelines. Remove staples and paper.

3 Using green yarn threaded through a needle, weave yarn in and out of holes on canvas. Keep stitches running in parallel rows, adding bells randomly. Leave a spot at the top of wreath to add a bow.

4 Place one end of a red ribbon at top of wreath, and tack it down. To tack, take threaded needle and push it through back side of canvas and ribbon. Leave 2 inches of thread on back side. Thread needle back down, going through ribbon, then canvas. Tie two loose threads on back of wreath in a knot.

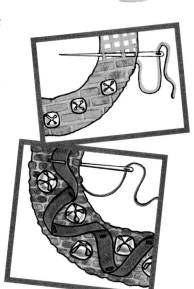

5 Continue tacking as you *loosely* twist and turn ribbon around bells. When ribbon meets back at the top, tack it down and cut off any excess. Make a pretty bow with extra ribbon and tack it to top of wreath.

6 To make backing and stand, cut a 4³/₄-inch circle out of cardboard. Spread craft glue along outer edge of cardboard, gluing only halfway around. Place this backing on wreath, with glued portion on bottom half of wreath. The photos will slide in and out of the top. Now cut a 2-by-4¹/₂-inch piece of cardboard for the stand. Measure 1 inch down from one end and crease. With craft glue, glue only this 1-inch section to backing, creating a stand. Let dry. Finally, insert your favorite pic and enjoy!

A SPECIAL CHRISTMAS TOUCH

It's easy to turn this decorative wreath into a hanging ornament. Instead of building a stand, take an 8-inch piece of yarn and loop it. Tape the two loose ends to the back of the frame at the top. Then hang your wreath from the nearest fir tree!

Christmas means family and friends. This wreath-shaped frame decorated with sleigh bells is the perfect way to display a holiday photo.

RANDOLPH, THE RAG-DEER

WHAT YOU'LL NEED

- scissors
- ruler
- 3-inch Styrofoam ball
- 1 yard light brown fabric
- six rubber bands
- raffia

- two twigs
- strong craft glue
- dark brown and red felt pieces
- one red pom-pom
- two black buttons

- straight pins
- red thread
- sewing needle
- six sleigh bells

DIRECTIONS

1 Cut twelve 1-by-36-inch strips from the light brown fabric. Drape all strips over the Styrofoam ball, and fan out the strips so that the ball is completely covered. Gather up all the strips and wrap them together with a rubber band tight against the Styrofoam ball. Make sure the ends of the dangling strips are about the same length.

2 Cut sixteen 1-by-14-inch strips from the brown fabric for the front legs. Divide the strips that are dangling from the Styrofoam ball in half. Slip the sixteen leg pieces between the split halves, making sure they are centered. Gather the two split halves back together and wrap with a rubber band right below the strips. This creates a waist and secures the front legs in place.

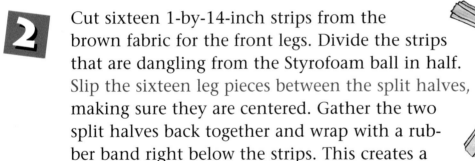

head
front legs
waist
back legs

3 Split the strips that are hanging below the waist in half to make the two back legs. Wrap a rubber band around each of the four ankles. To give your reindeer a fuller shape, flare out the strips on the legs and torso. Neatly trim the ends of the legs. Tie a few lengths of raffia around the ankles to cover the rubber bands.

4 Cut two 1-by-18-inch strips of brown fabric. Take one, wrap it twice around the neck, and tie it in a knot at the back. Repeat this with the second strip at the waist.

5 Ask an adult to make two "starter" holes in the top of the head using pointed scissors. Put a spot of glue into each hole and insert the two twig antlers.

6 Cut two teardrop shapes from the dark brown felt for the ears, and glue them onto the head just in front of the antlers. Glue on the red pom-pom nose and the two button eyes. You may wish to use straight pins to keep everything in place while dry- ing. Remove all pins once the glue is dry.

7 Cut a ¾-by-12-inch strip of red felt for the collar. Wrap it around the neck twice and glue it at the back. Trim any excess. With red thread, sew on three sleigh bells. Make a matching belt from a 1½-by-12-inch strip of red felt. Put it on at the waist, using the same directions as for the collar. Add the remaining bells, and Randolph is ready to fly!

A SPECIAL CHRISTMAS TOUCH

• • • • • • • • • • • •

Hang mini-ornaments from the rag-deer's antlers and find a fun place to display him for the holidays.

Here's a lovable, huggable reindeer made from gathered strips of fabric. With a sleigh-bell collar and a matching belt, he's ready to guide Santa's sleigh through the night!

THE MAGICAL SEE-THROUGH SNOWMAN

WHAT YOU'LL NEED

- two round balloons, 6 to 8 inches in diameter
- white crochet thread or kite string, 200 to 300 yards
- waxed paper
- liquid starch
- shallow pan

- paper towels
- two empty jelly jars
- needle
- scissors
- white cardboard
- strong craft glue

- crystal glitter craft paint
- two twigs
- black and orange felt
- fabric scrap
- cotton balls
- frosty glitter

DIRECTIONS

1 Inflate two round balloons, one slightly larger than the other. Knot balloons. Wrap each balloon with white crochet thread or kite string. Crisscross the thread in different directions. Be sure that the knots on the balloons stay free and clear from the wrapping.

2 Lay out waxed paper over your work surface. Pour enough liquid starch into a shallow pan to cover the bottom. Roll each balloon in the starch until the threads are saturated. Dab the balloons dry with paper towels and set each balloon on the open end of an empty jelly jar to dry overnight. Rotate the balloons a couple of times to ensure even drying. When dry, pop each balloon with a needle. Gently remove the balloons.

3 To make a base for your snowman, cut a 6-inch circle from the cardboard. Glue the bigger ball onto this circle, then glue the smaller ball on top. Paint the snowman with crystal glitter paint. Glue the two arm twigs into the sides of the body.

4 From black felt, cut a circle for the hat's brim. Cut out the center of this circle so that the hat will sit properly on the snowman's head. Cut a rectangle to be the hat's side and roll it into a cylinder. Glue it onto the brim. Cut a circle for the top and glue it on. When the hat is dry, glue it onto the snowman.

5 From orange felt, cut out a small triangle. Roll the triangle into a cone shape and glue it closed. From black felt, cut out eyes, mouth, and buttons. Glue all facial parts and buttons onto the snowman.

6 From your fabric, cut a piece for the scarf. Wrap the scarf around the snowman's neck and tie it in place. Put some glue onto the base. Shred up cotton balls and spread them out around the base. Add frosty glitter to the twig arms and portions of the hat.

This charming see-through snowman will "deck your halls" with delight . . . and he'll never melt! Now, that's magical!

A SPECIAL CHRISTMAS TOUCH

How about making a lady companion for your snowman? They make such a cute couple! She can wear a bow or a straw hat decorated with colorful silk flowers. (Little doll-size hats are available at most craft stores.)

CANDIED CANDLEHOLDER

WHAT YOU'LL NEED

- cardboard toilet paper roll
- cardboard scrap
- pencil
- scissors
- ruler

- 10-inch dinner candle
- aluminum foil
- red, green, or Christmas print wrapping paper
- strong craft glue

- four candy canes
- two rubber bands
- gold cording
- assorted hard candies (peppermints, lollipops, green and red candy)

DIRECTIONS

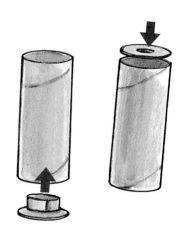

1 Place the toilet paper roll onto a piece of cardboard. Draw around the base of the core twice in separate spots. Cut out the two circles.

2 Now make the base for the candleholder. With a ruler, mark off a 1/2-by-3-inch rectangle. Cut it out, and wrap the strip around the candle so that the ring can slide on and off the candle bottom. Glue it closed. Glue the ring to the center of one of the circles, completing the base. Glue this base onto the toilet paper roll, with the ring on the inside. Cut a hole in the center of the remaining cardboard circle, big enough for the candle to pass through. Glue this piece to the top of the paper roll.

3 To make the top of the candleholder fire-resistant, cut a 3-inch circle from foil. Center the circle of foil over the top of your candleholder and flatten the foil down over the edges and onto the sides. Using a pencil, start a hole in the center of the foil. Poke your finger into the hole, and neatly tuck the foil inward around the opening.

4 Cut a 4-by-6-inch rectangle from wrapping paper. Spread glue on the plain side of the paper. Lining up the longer edge of the paper with the bottom of the holder, wrap the paper around it. There should be about a ½-inch rim of foil visible around the top of the rim.

5 Start decorating! Take four unwrapped candy canes and glue them upside down, spaced out around the sides. Use a small amount of strong craft glue when gluing on candies. If too much glue is used, the wet glue may dissolve the candy. Wrap rubber bands around the holder to keep everything in place while it's drying. If the glue is not dry after 24 hours, use a blow dryer to speed things up. Remove rubber bands once glue is dry. (If you can, have a parent help you use a low-heat glue gun on this step.)

6 If you use lollipops, tie bows of gold cord on the sticks. Or simply wrap and tie gold cord around the entire holder.

7 Glue on remaining unwrapped hard candies and lollipops. Finally, insert the candle into the holder. Push it in until the candle rests in the ring at the bottom. Remember: *Always* ask an adult to light a candle, and *never* leave a burning candle unattended!

This festive candleholder decorated with hard Christmas candies is sure to light up your holidays!

A SPECIAL CHRISTMAS TOUCH

Make a matching set of these delightful candleholders for the Christmas dinner table. They make sweet gifts, too!

HOLIDAY GIFT BAG

WHAT YOU'LL NEED

- one brown paper lunch bag
- glue
- cardboard, 3 inches by 5¼ inches
- ruler
- pencil
- hole puncher

- fabric of choice
- scissors with pointed tip
- red, beige, white, and black felt
- one white pom-pom
- twine
- tissue paper

DIRECTIONS

1 Glue the piece of cardboard to the inside bottom of the bag. Take the open end of the lunch bag and turn it out and over, creating a 2-inch "cuff."

2 To make holes for the handle, measure down ½ inch from the top of the folded cuff, and 1½ inches in from each side. Mark these spots with a pencil. Do this for both the front and back of the bag. Use a hole puncher and punch a hole at each pencil mark.

3 Cut a strip of fabric to cover the cuff of the bag, and glue it on. Once the glue is dry, with an adult's help, poke the point of the scissors through each of the four holes and the fabric.

4 Now you're ready to decorate your bag. You can copy one of the bags shown here or create your own original design. Glue the completed face or object onto the bag.

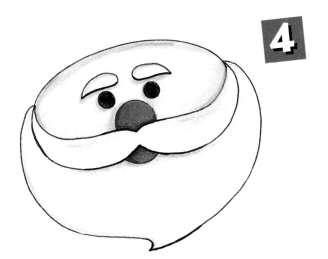

5 Cut two 12-inch lengths of twine. Take one and thread it through the holes in front of the bag, knotting the ends on the inside. Repeat this for the back handle. Use a spot of glue to keep the handles upright. Line the bag with tissue paper, and place your gift inside.

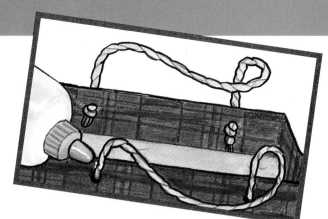

A SPECIAL CHRISTMAS TOUCH

Make a gift card. Take a 3-by-6-inch piece of poster board, fold it in half, and glue on a piece of matching fabric. Punch a hole and attach it to the gift bag with a loop of gold cord.

Transform a plain paper lunch bag into a merry gift bag decorated with your favorite Christmas character or theme.

SNOWFLAKE SWEATSHIRT

WHAT YOU'LL NEED

- dark-colored sweatshirt
- pencil
- ruler
- heavy-weight paper
- scissors
- waxed paper
- white fabric paint
- paper plate
- 1 inch square sponge scrap
- thin paintbrush
- crystal glitter fabric paint
- crystal rhinestones

DIRECTIONS

1 Wash and dry the dark-colored sweatshirt. Do not use fabric softener.

2 To make some snowflake stencils, draw an 8-inch square on a piece of heavy-weight paper. Centered inside this square, draw a smaller square measuring 5 inches. There should be a 1½-inch border around the 5-inch square. Cut out the 8-inch square.

1½"
5"
8"

3 Fold the square in half diagonally, with the pencil lines of the smaller square showing. Fold the form in half diagonally two more times.

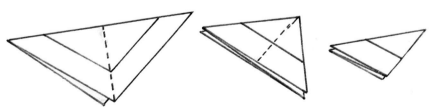

4 Using scissors, cut out a variety of shapes from the two folded-up sides, starting at the point. Be sure not to cut beyond the marked pencil line. When all the cutting is done, open up the square to reveal your snowflake stencil. Make two or three more stencils in smaller sizes and different patterns.

5 Line the inside of the sweatshirt with waxed paper and lay it out flat. Pour some white fabric paint onto a paper plate. Wet the sponge with water and squeeze out the excess water. Dab the sponge into the white paint, blotting off the excess paint. Place a snowflake stencil onto the sweatshirt. Using an up-and-down motion, dab the sponge all over the top of the stencil. Carefully remove the stencil.

6 Repeat step 5 using the snowflake stencils all over the sweatshirt and sleeves. If you want to decorate the back, wait until the front is dry, turn over, and stencil some more snowflakes.

You'll make quite a holiday fashion statement in this comfy sweatshirt decorated with frosty snowflakes.

7 With a paintbrush, add glitter paint to snowflakes to give them a "frosty" look. To attach rhinestones, squirt out a glob of glitter paint, and push the rhinestone down into it. Allow paint to dry.

A SPECIAL CHRISTMAS TOUCH

Decorate a ski cap, baseball cap, or other hat to match your sweatshirt. Or decorate a T-shirt and an old pair of jeans. What a fashionable way to keep toasty warm while you're dreaming of a white Christmas!

SINGING ANGEL CHIMES

WHAT YOU'LL NEED

- two small clay pots with 3½-inch-diameter tops
- small-to-medium-size paintbrushes
- craft paints, white and others of your choice
- modeling clay (polymer or fimo clay available at most craft stores)
- waxed paper
- rolling pin
- butter knife

- ruler
- pencil
- cookie sheet
- foil
- water-base clear sealer (latex urethane acrylic available at good paint stores)
- 1 yard of thick white cotton or nylon cord
- one gold metallic pipe cleaner

DIRECTIONS

 Paint the two clay pots, inside and out, with white paint. Once they are dry, apply a second coat.

 To make the clangor, take a piece of clay and roll it into a Ping-Pong-size ball. Stick a pencil all the way through it and set it aside.

 To make the hanging chime, roll more clay into another Ping-Pong-size ball. On a sheet of waxed paper, roll the ball out until it is about ¼ inch thick. Using a butter knife, cut the clay into a triangular shape with rounded corners, 2½ inches wide at the base and 3 inches tall. With a pencil, poke a hole through the top.

 With an adult's help, heat the oven to 250 degrees. Place the clay pieces onto a cookie sheet lined with foil. Bake them for two to five hours until they are hard. Ask an adult to remove the sheet from the oven when done, and allow pieces to cool.

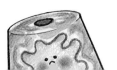

Sketch an angel face on one of the pots. Sketch in the arms and hands on the wide rim of the pot, and wings at the back. Paint it. The second pot is the angel's skirt. Paint a simple design around the hem.

Now paint the clangor and chime however you like. Once the paint is dry, brush on a coat of clear water-base sealer on all painted pieces. Allow pieces to dry.

To assemble your angel, tie on the flat chime to one end of the white cord. Make a tight knot and trim the short end of cord. Approximately 2½ inches up from the top of the chime, make a second knot. Thread the clangor onto the cord. Make a larger knot 2 inches up from the top of the clangor. Put the skirt pot onto the cord, open end over the clangor. Make one more large knot 2 inches up from the top of the skirt pot. Put on the angel's upper body so that it just overlaps the skirt pot.

To make a hanger for your chime, measure up 10 inches from the top of the head and loop the cord over. Secure the loop closed with a knot. Finally, crown your angel with a shimmering halo! Bend a metallic gold pipe cleaner into an "O," twisting the ends closed tight around the white cord above the angel's head.

Transform two clay pots into a heavenly angel full of song! She'll always sing as long as the breezes blow.

A SPECIAL CHRISTMAS TOUCH

Give your angel an extra long, flowing skirt of white satin ribbons. Simply glue lengths of ribbon to the inside of the bottom pot. The flowing ribbons will give your angel even more heavenly grace!

CANDY BAG ELF

WHAT YOU'LL NEED

- sandwich-size, non-zip plastic baggie
- assorted Christmas candy
- clear tape
- ruler
- scissors
- hole puncher (optional)
- 8-by-11-inch poster board
- 8-by-10-inch piece of green felt

- 3-by-3-inch squares of red, white, and skin-toned felt
- ½-inch size pom-poms (three red, five green)
- puff paints
- craft glue
- pencil

DIRECTIONS

1 Fill baggie with assorted Christmas candies. Twist top closed and wrap with clear tape. Set aside.

2 From poster board, cut out a rectangle 3 by 8 inches for main body and a 2-inch circle for head. On the rectangle, cut or punch a ⅜-inch hole positioned 1½ inches in from one end and centered as shown. Set aside.

3 From green felt, cut two 1-by-10-inch rectangles for arm pieces. Cut or punch a ⅜-inch hole at the center of both pieces.

4 Spread glue on one side of each of the two green felt pieces. Place the main body piece *perpendicular and on top of* one of the green felt pieces, lining up the holes. Align the second felt piece with the first, and attach it, glue side down, on top of the poster board. Again match the holes (see illustration).

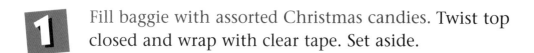

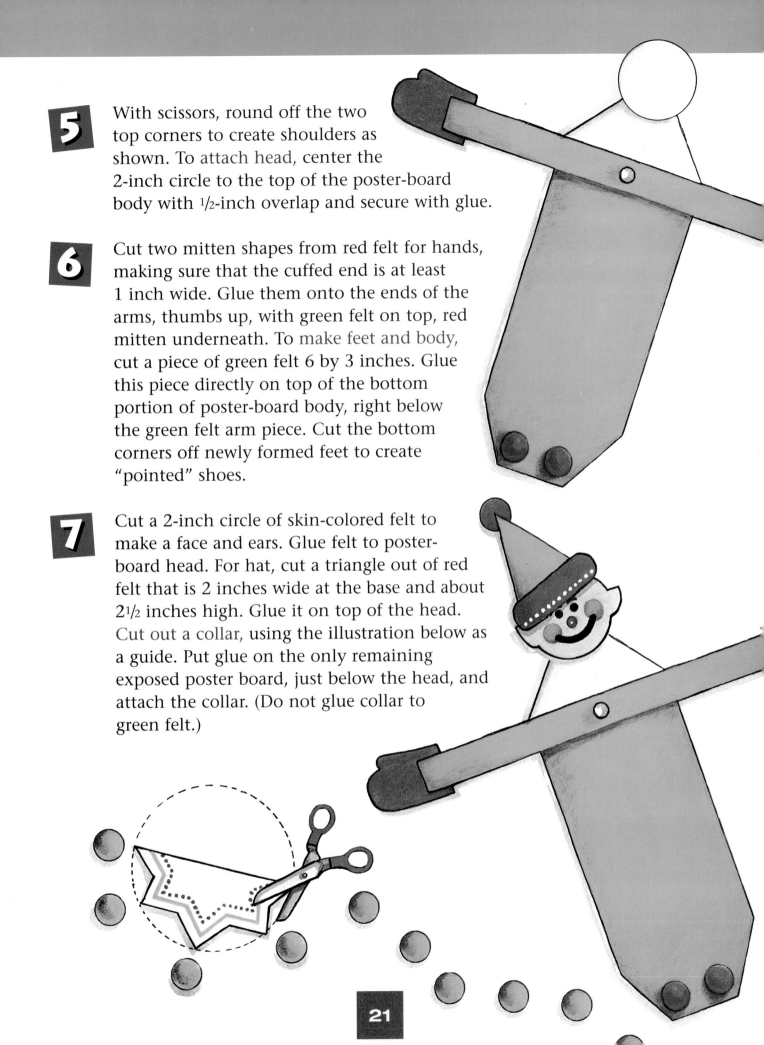

5 With scissors, round off the two top corners to create shoulders as shown. To attach head, center the 2-inch circle to the top of the poster-board body with ½-inch overlap and secure with glue.

6 Cut two mitten shapes from red felt for hands, making sure that the cuffed end is at least 1 inch wide. Glue them onto the ends of the arms, thumbs up, with green felt on top, red mitten underneath. To make feet and body, cut a piece of green felt 6 by 3 inches. Glue this piece directly on top of the bottom portion of poster-board body, right below the green felt arm piece. Cut the bottom corners off newly formed feet to create "pointed" shoes.

7 Cut a 2-inch circle of skin-colored felt to make a face and ears. Glue felt to poster-board head. For hat, cut a triangle out of red felt that is 2 inches wide at the base and about 2½ inches high. Glue it on top of the head. Cut out a collar, using the illustration below as a guide. Put glue on the only remaining exposed poster board, just below the head, and attach the collar. (Do not glue collar to green felt.)

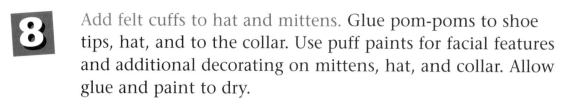

8 Add felt cuffs to hat and mittens. Glue pom-poms to shoe tips, hat, and to the collar. Use puff paints for facial features and additional decorating on mittens, hat, and collar. Allow glue and paint to dry.

9 To attach your merry little elf to his candy bag belly, take the twisted top part of the bag and pull it through the hole, now located under the collar. Spread craft glue on the palm side of the mittens. Bend the arms around the bag, attaching the hands to the front of the belly.

A SPECIAL CHRISTMAS TOUCH

Personalize your elf by replacing the elf face with a picture of a family member's face. Create a family of elves to represent your whole clan!

This merry little elf with a belly full of sugary treats makes a terrific holiday party favor or the perfect gift for your sweet-toothed pal.

AWAY IN A MANGER

WHAT YOU'LL NEED

- assorted sized wooden spools and wooden beads (available at most craft stores)
- glue
- craft paints
- small paintbrush
- scissors
- variety of scrap fabrics
- embroidery floss
- flat wooden toothpicks
- wire cutters
- gold cording
- aluminum foil
- assorted costume jewelry (rings, glass beads, and/or fake gems)
- cotton ball

DIRECTIONS

1 Select two wooden spools and two wooden beads and glue one wooden bead on top of each spool. You now have two complete little figures, Mary and Joseph. Allow glue to dry.

2 Paint the heads with a flesh tone and the bodies with colors of your choice. Paint two black dots for the eyes. Cut two fabric pieces to drape over the heads. Glue the fabric in place and trim if needed. Add a headband of embroidery floss on Joseph's head.

3 For Baby Jesus, glue a tiny bead for the head onto a tiny spool for the body. Allow glue to dry. Paint the head a flesh tone and the body white. Paint two black dots for the eyes. Cut a strip of white fabric and wrap it around the baby. Use a few dots of glue to keep it in place.

4 Assemble three bodies for the Wise Men by following step 1. For the Wise Men's arms, use the wire cutters to trim toothpicks to the desired length. Glue the arms onto the bodies. Allow glue to dry.

5 Paint the figures the desired colors. Cut strips of colorful fabrics for the Wise Men's robes and wrap them around each figure. Add sashes of embroidery floss or gold cording.

6 If you want a Wise Man to have hair, glue on strands of embroidery floss. Use your imagination for the headdresses and gifts. A crown can be made from a strip of foil. Gifts can be made from rhinestones and glass beads. Glue crowns and gifts to figures.

7 To build the drummer boy, select two tiny spools to make up his body. Glue one spool horizontally (on its side) on the top of the other. Glue a small wooden bead on top of the body for a head. Add arms, clothes, and hair as you did for the Wise Men. Paint a tiny spool for the drum and glue it to the front of the boy's body. Make two tiny drumsticks from pieces of toothpick, and glue them onto the drummer boy's hands.

8 Animals such as sheep, cattle, and camels are made by gluing spools of various sizes together. Legs, ears, and horns are made from lengths of toothpicks glued on. Let legs dry before turning the animal over and attaching horns and ears.

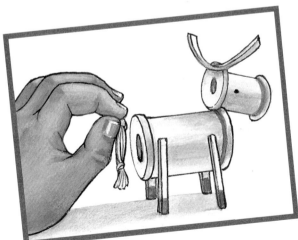

The true spirit of Christmas is captured in this charming mini-manger scene made from wooden spools, beads, and toothpicks.

9 Paint animals the desired colors. Shred up a cotton ball and glue it around the lamb's body for fleece. A few strands of embroidery floss can be glued onto a steer for a tail. You can also make an animal lie on the ground by not giving it legs.

A SPECIAL CHRISTMAS TOUCH

Design a manger using a shoe box decorated with Spanish moss, twigs, scraps of weathered wood, bark, rocks, and pine needles. And don't forget the Star of Bethlehem! Use your imagination and have fun!

SCENTED CHRISTMAS STOCKING

WHAT YOU'LL NEED

- child's sock
- cinnamon-scented potpourri
- needle and thread
- scissors
- Christmas print fabric
- strong craft glue
- ribbon, cording, pom-poms, small sleigh bells, and rickrack trims
- fabric paint with a writer tip

DIRECTIONS

 Fill the sock with potpourri. Using a needle and thread, sew the top closed. To make a cuff for the stocking, cut a rectangle from the Christmas print fabric. Glue the fabric around the top of the sock.

 Add trimming to the cuff. Be creative! You can glue on ribbons, cording, rickrack, pom-poms, and sleigh bells. You'll need to sew on the sleigh bells because of their weight.

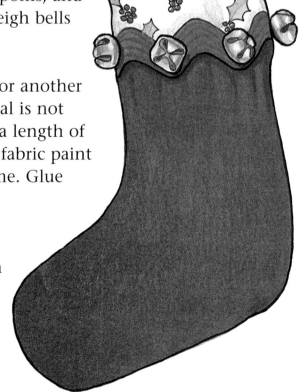

3 Personalize the stocking with your own or another special person's name. If the sock material is not smooth enough surface to write on, cut a length of ribbon and write the name on that. Use fabric paint in a writer-tip bottle to paint on the name. Glue the ribbon onto the stocking.

 To decorate the rest of the sock, cut out some designs from the fabric. Glue them onto the stocking.

5 To make a hanger, sew a loop of cording or ribbon onto the top of the stocking.

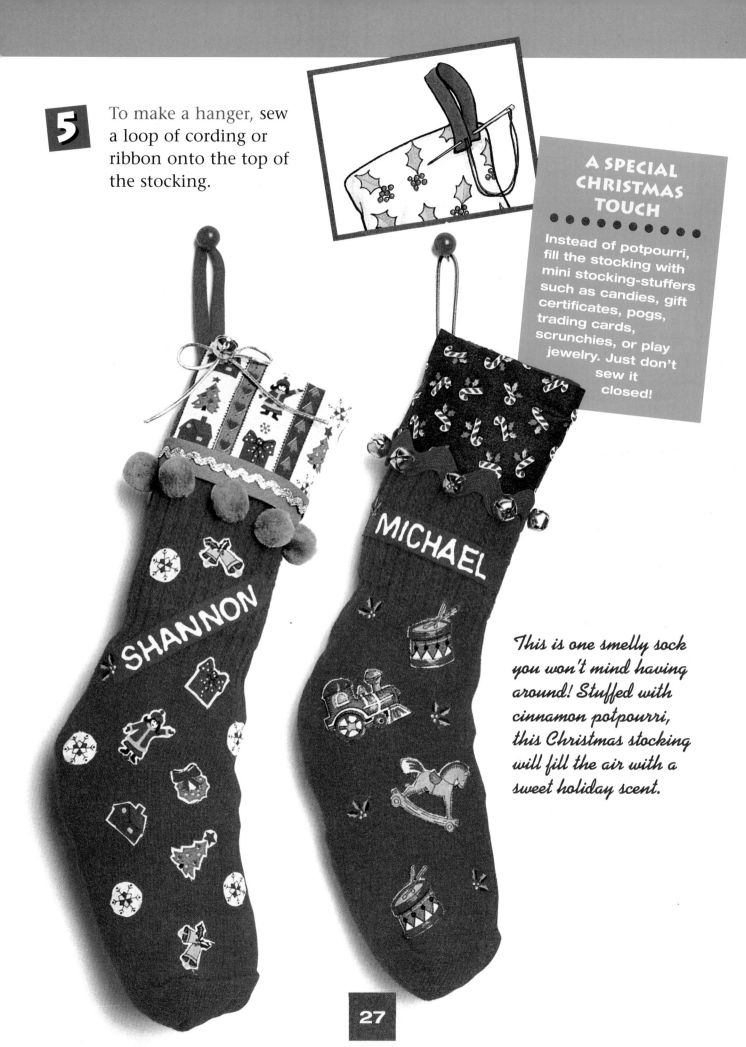

A SPECIAL CHRISTMAS TOUCH

Instead of potpourri, fill the stocking with mini stocking-stuffers such as candies, gift certificates, pogs, trading cards, scrunchies, or play jewelry. Just don't sew it closed!

SHANNON

MICHAEL

This is one smelly sock you won't mind having around! Stuffed with cinnamon potpourri, this Christmas stocking will fill the air with a sweet holiday scent.

CHRISTMAS TREE CARD HOLDER

WHAT YOU'LL NEED

- ruler
- pencil
- one piece medium-weight cardboard, 24 inches by 30 inches
- scissors
- strong craft glue
- cotton batting

- 1 yard Christmas print fabric
- gold, red, or green metallic elastic cord
- yellow foam sheet (available at most craft stores) or yellow felt

DIRECTIONS

1 Draw a triangle on the cardboard, 24 inches at the base and 30 inches high. Cut it out.

2 Starting at the top point, measure down one side of the triangle 6 inches and draw a horizontal line across the tree. From that line, continue down the triangle, drawing horizontal lines every 2½ inches until you have nine lines. Cut ¼-inch-deep notches along the two sides where each horizontal line meets the edge.

3 Turn the triangle over so that the lined side is face down. Put glue all over the surface of the triangle, then cover it with a thin layer of batting.

4 Cut a triangle from the fabric, 28 inches at the base and 34 inches high. Place the fabric flat on a work surface, wrong side up. Place the cardboard triangle, batting side down, on top of the fabric. Wrap the fabric edges over and glue them onto the back, lined side. Allow glue to dry.

5 Wrap nine elastic cords around the tree, trapping each one in the notches. Tie the cords tightly at the back. A couple of spots of glue on each cord at the back will help to keep them in place.

6 From a yellow foam sheet or felt, cut a star and glue it to the top of the tree. Hang your Christmas cards from the cords.

Here's a delightful and fun way to display the Christmas cards you receive from family and friends.

A SPECIAL CHRISTMAS TOUCH
• • • • • • • • •
As you hang more and more Christmas cards on your tree, they will overlap each other, creating a wonderful design all their own.

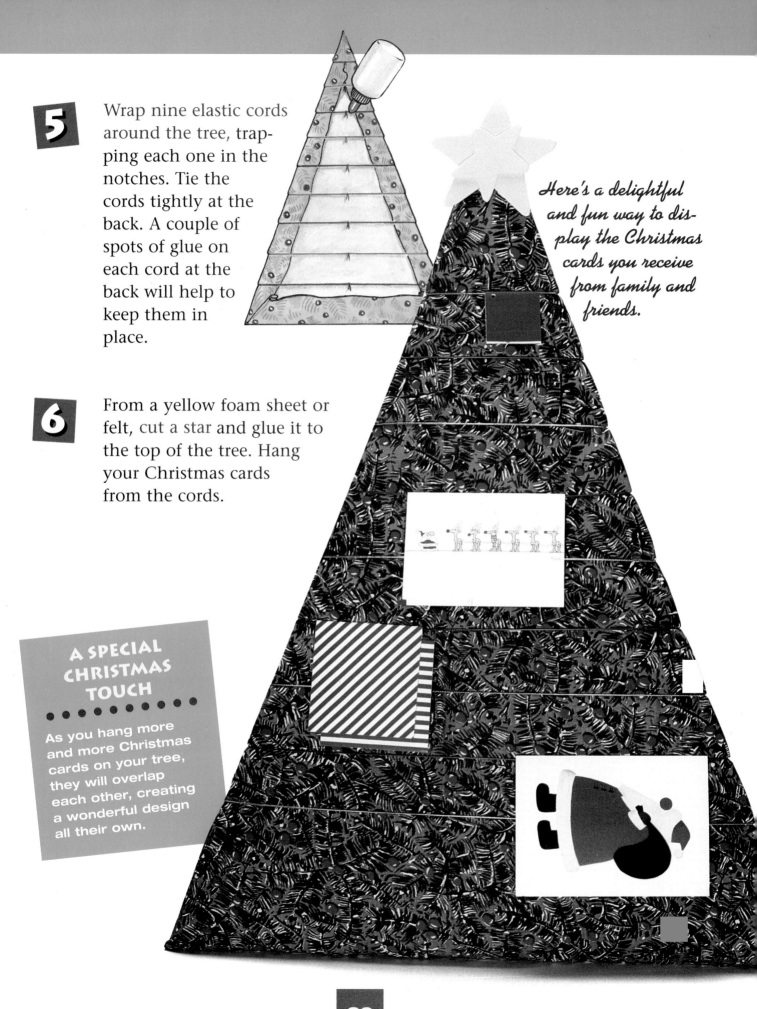

GINGERBREAD COTTAGE KEEPSAKE BOX

WHAT YOU'LL NEED

- cube-style tissue box
- ruler
- pencil
- scissors
- poster board
- colorful foam sheets (available at most craft stores) or felt

- masking tape
- crystal glitter paint
- holiday print fabric
- miniature plastic ornaments such as candy canes, gingerbread men, and stars (optional)

DIRECTIONS

 Measure down 2 inches from the top of a cube tissue box, and make a pencil line all the way around. Cut the tissue box along this line. Keep the bottom half and discard the top.

2 On the poster board, draw two triangles measuring 4³/₈ inches at the base and 2 inches high. The two sides should measure 3 inches in length. On the 3-inch side, draw tabs ½ inch wide. Cut out the two triangles.

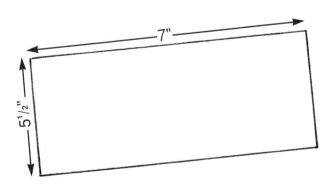

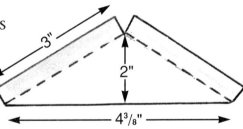 To make the rooftop, draw a rectangle measuring 7 inches by 5½ inches on poster board. Cut out the rectangle.

4 Fold the rectangle in half, creating two 3½-by-5½-inch rectangles. Fold down the tabs and glue them on the two triangles into the "V" of the rooftop. Glue the triangles ½ inch in from the edge of the roofline to create an overhang.

5 Start decorating with the roof half. Cut out a white piece of foam, 7 inches by 5½ inches. Glue the foam onto the rooftop. If foam sheets cannot be found, felt can be used as a substitute.

6 From light brown foam, cut out two triangles to fit the two sides of the rooftop. Glue them on. Also cover the bottom half of the cottage with light brown foam. Do the front and two sides only, leaving the back alone.

7 Add a door, windows, shutters, and candies from shapes out of the colorful foam sheets. Glue them onto your cottage. If you have any miniature ornaments such as candy canes, gingerbread men, or stars, glue them on now.

8 It's time to connect the roof to the cottage. Place the roof half on top of the cottage and put a few pieces of masking tape lengthwise on the outside and inside of the back wall where the two halves meet. Cut a piece of light brown foam to cover the entire outside back of the cottage. Glue it on.

9 Decorate the back of the cottage. Add touches of crystal glitter paint to some of the candy to give them a "sugary" look. Line the inside of your cottage with a festive holiday print fabric, gluing the fabric to the cardboard with fabric glue. Use your gingerbread cottage to store holiday jewelry, candies, or small knickknacks.

A SPECIAL CHRISTMAS TOUCH

Make a whole Christmas village scene using different-size boxes. Decorate each house differently. You can even cover the ground with cotton batting and make trees and shrubs out of tissue paper and twigs.

This quaint gingerbread cottage is made from a tissue box. Maybe a special holiday surprise awaits inside!